The Inland Sea

BARRY HILL's long narrative poem, *Ghosting William Buckley* won the 1994 NSW Premier's Award for Poetry, and his labour history, *Sitting-In* won the same award for Non-Fiction in 1992. He is the winner of other national awards for non-fiction and works for radio. His short fiction has been widely anthologised and translated. Although he lives by the sea in Queenscliff, Victoria, his recent work, including *The Inland Sea*, his third book of poetry, arises out of travelling and research in Central Australia. His most recent book is *The Rock: Travelling to Uluru*. He teaches occasionally at the University of Melbourne and is poetry editor for the national newspaper, *The Australian*.

The Inland Sea

Barry Hill

SALT

PUBLISHED BY SALT PUBLISHING
PO Box 202, Applecross, Western Australia 6153
PO Box 937, Great Wilbraham, Cambridge PDO CB1 5JX United Kingdom

First published 2001
Reprinted 2002

Printed and bound in the United Kingdom by Lightning Source

Typeset in Swift 9.5 / 13

British Library Cataloguing-in-Publication Data
A catalogue record for this book is available from the British Library
ISBN 1 876857 27 7 paperback

SP

1 3 5 7 9 8 6 4 2

To Ramona

Let our sweet sap ooze from the ground
Let our dark honey ooze from the ground

BANDICOOT SONG OF ILBALINTJA
T. G. H. STREHLOW

When a man is together with his wife
the longing of the eternal hills blows around them

MARTIN BUBER

When you understand
that my poems really aren't poems
Then we can talk poetry together

ZEN MASTER RYOKAN

Contents

Acknowledgements

In the last sentence of his great book, *Songs of Central Australia* (1971 Angus and Robertson) T. G. H. Strehlow looked to the day when Australian verse might be woven on "the poetic threads spun on the Stone Age hair-spindles of Central Australia." I believe I have used Aranda lines in the spirit of that thought, and the few that I have cited have been previously published in 'Welcoming Dance' *Overland* Autumn 1992. For the full passage of kangaroo eating see *Aranda Phonetics and Grammar*, Oceania Monograph No. 7 p108–9. For the *Song of Songs* see, mainly, Marvin H. Pope (*The Song of Songs*. The Anchor Bible. Doubleday 1977), Michael V. Fox (*The Song of Songs and the Ancient Egyptian Love Songs*. University of Wisconsin Press 1985), and Ariel and Chana Bloch (*The Song of Songs*. Random House New York 1995).

Versions of some of these poems have been published in *Island* Summer 1996, *Meanjin* 2, 2001, *refo* 4, 2001, and *Boxkite* 4, 2000, and on the Australian Broadcasting Commission's *The Listening Room* February, 2001.

Many thanks also to Martin Harrison, Beverley Farmer and Mike Ladd whose scrutiny assisted this manuscript at different stages of its life; to John Wolseley, who let me borrow his image of the honey increase centre at Ewaninga; to Peter Latz, whose home was so often my base in Alice Springs, and upon whose wall a version of the Ewaninga work hung.

Part One

Song

O
let him
           drink me
           with his kisses

Your loving is sweeter than wine

Your scent
myrrh and aloes
Your name is perfume
           No wonder
           the young women want you

Yapalpa

I sit in his shadow desiring,
and its fruit is sweet to my taste.

He brings me to his banquet hall
raises the banner of love over me

O feed me up with raisins
plump me with apples
for I am limp with love.

With his left hand he cups my head
and with his right hand
he embraces me.

MAN

Your eyes are doves.

Your hair flocks
in the gorge of Yapalpa.

You are a fountain of gardens
a well of living waters

You are the loveliest of women
without blemish.

Beauty you are my bride.
Your love is sweeter than wine
your scents are sweeter than spices
your lips my bride are honeycomb,
milk and honey under your tongue.
Your dress is as aromatic as this whole, central place.

WOMAN

I was asleep but my heart woke.
Let my love come into his garden
and eat his precious fruits

MAN

I have come into my garden, my bride

Bringing the *Song of Songs* into our wedding service, what was I
doing?

Placing the Hebrew lotus beside the Buddha's.

Floating the flower on the ancient pool of Yapapla, a place of
genesis in Central Australia.

Planting one desert in another desert.

In the haplessness of translation, in the hope of love.

Nectar

Eating honey ant
is tasting bitterness
at first,
       you put
the tail on your tongue,
         acrid tip to acrid tip, then
you put the living thing
         further in.
A golden bubble
         like a promise
swells behind your teeth.
          Expectant,
you have filled
your mouth with the idea
         of sweetness.
But there is nothing to compare
with this bursting
         that is to each taste and
which is as it dissolves
a tear
         of nectar.

Noon

Blues in their eyes burn
in ether of patience, strange sacrifice.

Both endure their trance
of solid starlight. No

rock in shadow
all days exposed.

In this antique, inland sea
obligation is shedding its skin.

And still she is swollen with honey,
she glistens with gift and trust.

Ribs

There are
  wave formations
      in the archaic rocks.
  Fish ripple
  in shoals of salt.

In the
  throbbing heat,
              a gauze
  dressed all wounds
  renamed the hours.

Satellite photographs
  show blue blood,
      thinking veins all over:
  bodies of song
  in ribs of ranges.

This place
  is made
      for matrimony.
  It is laid out
  in trust in time.

Chant
  and snakes
      are rainbows.

Nuptial Rocks

Cannibalism and granite.
Flesh and rock.
Pre-historic undulations
devour time. Ridges lie
In bones of the dead.

We pick and lope our way.
One step,
on stone as pink
as your mouth,
another on
lilac and date-coloured chips
—the treasures of the gorge
listening like Solomon.

Rose song.
Song of lilac and date.
All the old mineral lilts.
Boulders in honeyed sands.
Slabs sluiced as altars.
Along the milk-white river bed
glints of sacrifice.

Pale
perfumed
with open hands,
we are where a wallaby sits
alert as a vow
ash-pawed
quivering.

Little Buddha

And the Buddha by the pool.
My small one, of soap stone.
A smooth semblance of
heaven within the mountain.
Gentle as a duck feather
floating under the full moon.

It saw. We heard. The gorge,
wide as protoplasmic Dreaming,
listened to all the old words
seethed open into ancestry.
Out of the corner of my eye
green rushes weaved their dance.

Would we leave it there?
I was happy enough to let it go,
turn my back on a graven image,
all for you. As you had sweetly stood
with the icon of the other shore.
Both surrendered by that pool.

Later the photos said it all.
Watery images. Cloud and warm water swirls
as translucent as the self.
As overlapping in time and space.
As inclusive, yes.
Your hair, your white, blue dress;
my shoulders and throat gone floral.

And the little Buddha spectre:
double-exposed with crocodile.
His calm smile in the tail.
A row of teeth in his lap.
How things happen hardly matters.
What swims in time is true
when you enter a pool with vows.

Dove

In the clear light of the desert autumn
    in the teeth of the gorge lit from within
where granite quivers in mauve and purple
    where the baking range is a loaf of time
where you can walk right into a cave
    and paint your body throbbing with ochre
where wide flat stones have been rubbed smooth
    and are as settled as dusk for the callused foot
where flesh will be as healed as emerald reeds
    where the snake lolls in the ripples of duck
spreading its thoughts thinly, its belly yellow
    where water lives, and pigment breeds
where no being stirs, where all were born—
place your feet in the pool,
    saying *Rain*, saying *Dove*

Song

WOMAN

> Lotus I am
>> a wild one
>> in the valley

MAN

> A lotus you are
>> among the thorns
>> of other women.

WOMAN

> Apricot
>> a tree of the wood
>> my love surpasses others
> I sit in his shade desiring
>> its sweet crop to my taste.
>> He brings me to his house of wine,
> raises the banner of love over me.

> O feed me up
>> with raisins
>> plump me
> with apricots
>> bed me among fruits
>> I am fevered with love.

Banquet

You are such a beauty.
Layers keep coming off us.
Skins. Luscious peelings of surprise
so that even when you are gone
hours later, and my hands,
for those dumb reasons of a day,
must be wiped of you,
and when your face ripening
over/ under mine no longer
glows in my inward gaze,
I am like some native yam
like your regular home-grown tuber
that sugar/ starch tropical root
food—still swollen for you:
and swelling as I say this
mouthful after mouthful.

Part Two

Song

I say to myself now:
    I will climb up
        into the palms
I will seize its branches
    and let your breasts bunch
        as dates.
Your breath
    the apricots
        your mouth
            the best wine.

Caravan

1

Light rippling the slim white branches.
　　　A grasshopper, hungry husk, leaps
towards its drum, belly full of summer's hum.

　　　And *Jilpi* Possum in the caravan there
under the lovely young woman tree.
　　　You can see his shadow, the bottle
of water to his lips—no family here for Possum,
　　　　free to leave the grog
alone as much as he likes.
　　　His head then out of sight,
gone into his laid-out paintings
　　　　in the shade of the young woman tree.

It is so quiet you can hear the breathing leaves.
　　　A pale lemon, like the pink,
goes on with feathery firmness:
　　　　it's nothing, the way the heavy
earth brown is slowly patched
　　　　over with a lilac
and the fridge's little old motor
　　　　goes quiet for the next daub,
a cool bird in distant shade.

　　　I'm having a good sit down
my note book is over there.
　　　Love to get a lemon like that
on the page! Don't worry
　　　　don't ask about it,
the ground's a tarp for rain,
　　　　might come tonight, might not
wait and see the lilac
　　　　as a jigsaw shape
one meeting the other
　　　　under the lovely young woman tree.

Don't live here, come back when I can.
　　Rest the harp in the caravan.
Let the seasons blow through the mesh,
　　my hand on the snib
　　　of the tender door.

2

Wind in the north again.
Memory of childhood shortens my breath.
       Did you marry me?
Already my eyes are streaming.

       Last night, thunder
and sheet lightning. For a while
       the wind went round to the south.
I was walking by the sea
       breathing easily, you on my arm.
Then, sometime before dawn, dreaming
       I had returned from a trip
you were there, you had been

       waiting for my return,
smoking a lot of dope.
       What I'd been doing I don't know,
but I had come back
       to ask you if it was
good, still good, with
       my cheek against yours
in these noon gusts
       the heat now.

       Birds flit at the memories of moisture.
Honey eaters, their yellow beaks
       pepper the corkwood, pigeons
flick in the dust. Two pink galahs
       calm on the broken acacia
know better and alight for the range.
       Dug out again, the day returns
       to the wide sky.

       A crow makes a quick call
near my rock. Off! Just what
       we should do with fright.
Off, off with naked fear, what
       does it matter if one or other

of us, both of us, must be
	alone all over again.
Albatrossed. Imagine!
	All manner of birds come
to mind in the new breeze.

	Oh it matters
it matters as much as food, as air
	that we stay together.
Holy is the bird soaring
	on hot winds with hope.

By midday
	all pieties come to a dead stop.
That's what happens
	in the vineyard
	when the shade of a stupor
has overtaken you:
	your sleep is not even the sleep
of the wicked.

	It is a nothing,
	a heavy-lidded eddy
of indifference, even to pleasure.
	I might wake fine, looking for chocolate,
but the old songs do me no good:
	they are as mute as the chorus
	when the Shulamite was most glorious
—uncovering a man's eyes.

3

That tree,
       that beautiful tree.
Wonder if Possum will paint it.
       At dusk she eases back
against the range, preparing to receive
       the birds, the glowing
fat trunk heaves welcome,
       in pink blur and raucous
lack of appreciation
       they fall upon her.
Screeches scar
       pale limbs until dark.

In the full sap of night she listens.
       I lie beside her
owlish and adrift.
       In her composure,
those full assemblies of leaves,
       all our thoughts of the day
rustle quietly, brush stars.

   ·   She is the kind of tree
that salaams to daylight
       with yoga breath,
is a psalm to morning
       and honey eaters:
so sweet in what seems,
       day after day to be
a youthful amplitude,
       that I agelessly want
to sing out, hug her girth
       beat time at her base
paw her roots.

       Instead I wait.
She whispers and sways
       also expectant.
A shoulder bare

to the serpentine light
is so white that it hurts.
In mid-morning ecstasy
her whole body writhes.
It is as if she is sentinel
to a company of happy
women seasonally arriving:
hair down, their breasts
oiled and bearing
the glaze of resin.

She's as tall as she is wide.
Her compass measures flood.
Her height is lunar.
She looks down on
the glory of wattle
is insouciant
towards the nectar of corkwood
and emu bush
that green which lactates men.

נֹפֶת תִּטֹּפְנָה שִׂפְתוֹתַיִךְ כַּלָּה

Ngkwarle

Your lips are honey, honey and milk

Sweet foods like honey

Their sweet dark juice is flowing forth;
From the centre of the chalice is flowing forth

From the slender pistil it is flowing forth;
The sweet dark juice is flowing forth

Let our sap encircle them with rings;
Let the flood of nectar encircle them

Let our sweet sap ooze from the ground. . . . .

High blown—Strehlow's diction in *Songs of Central Australia.*

As a lover of antiquity, a seeker of eternity, he was in tune with the Hebrew habit of couplets, where the lines lie parallel with each other, one arm around the other, in skillful repetition.

The golden braid that couplets make as they dance down a page.

His translations rooted him in this place, as a love of love watered the *Song of Songs.*

The translator as celebrant.

Song

See—
beside a wall he stands
shows himself
glancing through the lattice.
And he speaks to me:
Rise my love, he says,
loveliest woman come.
Winter is done.
The rains are over
our land is blooming.
All the singing birds are here
even the turtledove.
The fig sweetens its young fruit
with fragrance vine buds are
dripping my love—
rise loveliest woman, come
my dove in the cleft
of the rock
latticed in your covert
let me see
let me hear your voice
your sweet voice

Desert Cradling

This morning, for safe keeping, on the way back to you,
I wrapped my Buddha in my kipah (the one your father gave me).
It surprised me there so long after Passover—
folded into my top jacket pocket, hidden cargo for this journey
that calls for the Buddha, as everything does in silken wedlock.

A plush kipah, royal blue with gold-braid, flesh-coloured lining.
It is new to my crown but not unbecoming
though I sit under it less often than I sit on
the meditation mat. *Om Mani Padme Hum.*
Jewel in the Crown of the Lotus. Repeat it
in retreat and after one thousand minutes or years
or in an instant body, speech and mind clears:
sitting sings rather than aches: the chant fits.

In the song that landed us here, the *kipah*,
as light on the head as a bell bird, can't help,
(the sky is too wide, the country too hot
for an indoor hat), but at Passover
when I do wear it, I hope it is
as deserved as this love from you
or as the long vineyard of the moment
when I gather myself up from the mat,
awakened for freedom, and the fankincensed full silence,
when the original tongue is the host tongue,

and the head is a wonderful thing, again—
the way it receives adornments,
at pujas women wear painted scarves,
men flowers if they desire there is no end . . .
Here, by the ancient river,
near the glowing sandstone cliff
embossed with snake that guards the snake,
duck feathers or eagle down, head band of red twine—
all may be aides to the space-time journey

called marriage. Starting out along the river bed,
in the white sand, in the elephantine shade of coolabahs,
—those Ganesh trees that dance for cyclones and stand
to protect millennial memories—we move in rock heat,
in a trance as grand as the cedars of Lebanon. Thus

our beginning near the green pool, where the dove
landed, and we removed each other's head cover
each evening after the day's travelling, a coo
in my throat at last, a breasting peace in my voice,
creating a gentle berth for my sharp tongue.

Feathers of wind along the river all night.
You could open your eyes to the Milky Way
see the river beyond rivers in the mists of light
from where the first-born fell, and gills of time trembled.

There was one night, yes, when we couldn't sleep.
Muggy. Cattle lowering. And a donkey's heated braying.
The more it heaved the more the moon waxed for it.
From our own stickiness we'd heaved apart almost
surely at union, and then, parched and flouting creature-
        knowledge
I mounted you again, and sure enough the dingo

bitch was back, emboldened and coal-eyed, stalking our fire
as if meat was still in it. We guffawed her off, she slunk
along the river to her over-licked mate and litter
but a night meant for union had soured, the itch
of the camp breathed a promise of rain, a downpour
at the wrong time of year, but what's the wrong time
for a row when it pours? I'd hated your love
of that moon. You gazed at its drifting face and hated

my meditation cold. We broke camp in good time
what ever good time is . . . for love, for daylight, even, finally
for the desert deluge and its random stopping.
In the larger scheme of things you have to say,
'the rain has eased off, that's all', like fire when
droplets of oil in the virile spinifex flare, and
dry grass leaps into flame and dies in dust somewhere.

Sulking, I know—like a mosquito—my blood.
Then I am feasted and limp at your wrist, having come to,
out of myself, when you only need your speaking voice,
its succouring warmth and shine, its dread-filled lilt.
What's our record for cold shoulders on opposite banks?
For being stock still with quartz heart. A day? A year?
Each mineral streak hardens misery until
as every traveller knows, the waterhole is gained only by

kneeling at it. One moment
—was the rift a moment?—
each slab in the gorge gleaming purple vengeance
next I have put the plush little cap on, you've
found the lotus and we are drinking each other with black
cockatoos fanning the water, squawking that pride
pride can't matter, not in the end, the end.

My time here says meditation is rock,
and the surfacing of secret life-saving rivers horses can sniff
called soaks. What does it take to marry underground?
For honey-ant nectar to wash the mouth of bitterness?
What it takes for a place to shift from singular grieving slabs,
to bands of red-ochred mindfulness of each others headpiece!
You crossing from Egypt and coming towards me in freedom.
Me still trying to balance in Emptiness, the porous trust
of our desert cradling, from water to water, silken and bound.

WOMAN

I am my love's love
and his desire is me.

Come my love let us go
        into the fields
        into the vineyards
        for the whole night.
Let us see if the vines
        have flowered
        their blossoms opened
        their pomegranate burst.
There I will give you all my love.
        Mandrakes exude their scent
        in the doorway
there are all fruits
        all manner of fruits
        old and new
that I have laid up for you.

The great sire, proud and handsome
Burns a fiery yellow.

I am a married man, a truly married man
I am full of joy in my wife.

I am full of love for my wife;
I am a married man, a truly married man.

T. G. H. STREHLOW: *Song of the Kwalba Chief of Tera.*

At Babel Bore

See the camels browsing
    in their field.
        Loping solemnly through scrub
limbs rhythmic
    as seasons
        each plump fold of their haunches
patient about water
    their haughtiness
        reserved for newcomers
to their garden,
    no touch of hubris, really,
        more a matter of knowing
a desert other than this one
    while lacking the means
        to say.

Anyway
    there they were
        snaffling
the upper reaches of shrubs
    gliding up the bowers of acacia
        fresh leaf of whitewood
flower of beefwood. Gardening.
    Well, after a fashion.
        They are in the garden of the clan.

See the end
    of the afternoon now
        every new leaf
in bloom of glint
    the spinifex so luminous
        it's love food
they munch
    upwards away from
        those painful ground-cover needles,
treat a treetop
    with the reverence

of a sacred text:
they graze along the line
     like rabbis
         or monks with their
seed syllables.
     Hungers eternal.

I approach slowly
     in the afternoon glow
         in the ancient light
that baked pyramid
     and serpentine reach of
           brontosaurus
necks as thick as time
     gentle as water.
         I craned to see
wishing you with me—
     We get a glimpse
         sometimes
not of love through slats
     which stops the heart for a second,
         but of the archaic
from horizon to horizon,
     the sightings of mountains
         hurled from ice
hatched from jungle,
     of lakes, seas,
         all of them inland.
Babble Bore.
     place for thirsty singing
         thus a source
for all songs but
     in this desert there's
         no tabernacle
of nouns;
     the abstract tends to burn
         out in a day;
you see the wisps of cirrus
     and maybe a build up
         of alto-stratus;

the wind is in the west at last
  but still nothing happens
    because this configuration
is not it when
  there's no more to it
    than there is one way
for a camel to reach
  Babble Bore:
    they come in lines that
crisscross, intersect,
  stray and loop
    around the loose definition

of this great 'paddock'
  they've been herded into:
    they are kin based
on their particular
  latitude, the vicissitudes
    of their own Greenwich,
as in:
  your hair,
    how is that now
exactly
  what freedom
    did you give it this morning,
what air breathes through it,
  what scent
    was it washed in?
the more scent
  the better for a man
    to babble into,
every curl of it
  on your walk towards his well
    to break the drought
of waiting.

So.
At Babel Bore
  the camels were
    in the open air.

The same bulls
        cows
                spindly youths.
Devil
        Olive
                White One
And the one I'll call
        for the sake of hindquarters
                plumpness
and endearment—
        Leah . . .
                Well, why not,
dear 'wild cow'—
        who sits as sweet as a lotus,
                she's closest to an unnamed one
I want to call Dog
        because he's nearest to
                that dingo in the shade
closest to me.
        Dog and dingo kinship
                at Babel Bore
making its own song
        in the stunning heat
                of necessity,
where the world waits
        nothing stands up
                except sounds
of mud cracking
        like clap sticks
                dancing feet . . .
Why, it is a musical
        shade
                I can sit on the top
of the Toyota
        thicken my throat
                in dusty rumble
get the sound rolling
        after Devil as he lopes
                with a mind to Olive
her head aslant

[36]

at my wild
                seed syllables—
I can do so if
        I've had my fill
                of water and they theirs,
if we can agree to
        strike up song together,
                running it back through
scrub, between
        the lovely sad casuarinas,
                along the fading lilac
line of salt lake
        to the next rise where
                limestone breaks out
in pink puck eyed ground,
        and singing resounds
                for underground travelling

notes for bones
        melody for waters,
                I can growl my princely
camel call and they know
        lion and springy goat,
                gazelle and leopard;
my voice reaches them
        in desert dialogue.

Swart but beautiful my throat sounds.
They drink it up on the run.

Song

My beloved
> *has gone down*
> *into the garden*
> *into his beds of spices*

to graze there
> *and to gather lotus.*
> *I am his love and he is mine.*
> *He feasts among the lotus.*

One day we walked together, out on the salt lake.

Come on, I said, this way.

We were still in love, I think.

Footsteps, like words found in translation, led us towards the
centre.

Except, as in translation, no centre was possible; it could not be
reached, word by word.

Behind us was some notion of the original.

Out there, towards the middle, the crust gave way.

Very slowly we had to turn back.

But we pressed on around the salt lake, stepping lightly on the
succulents.

Salts

1

She is speaking
amorously of abstractions
sunlight in her hair, weaving and woven,
one concept into another, sets and sets
an orb for her crown of equations,
as if her logic is guiltless, free,
she's smiling and playing with parenthesis
for the joyous child within
spindle and wheel of Reason;
Gestalt at full tilt in her voicing
of Nature in Mind, Mind in Nature,
in the total, gentle, circumstance of morning.

It's a matter, she says
—the northern light behind her—
of thresholds. You can have
too much of anything, from calcium
to psychotherapy. What counts is the whole
design as it arranges itself, more and less,
according to the fields we're in.

Or so to speak. I am speaking here.
'I' the other weaving lines
from the lap of her unfurling,
her strands of exposition, each thought
flicked and held—or almost held—
by comb after comb of wave formations
as particled as salt: crystals in the foam
of time's ocean of thought

with her hair—
even as she speaks
curling and tossed, glittering
in sea sprays of concept.

2

Later, as if heavy-hearted from the sea,
She turns, and walks inland,
fairness billowing the onshore breeze.

I watch her pass
under our coastal gums, her shadow lengthen
by the poplars, a figure

diminished in blues
within blues, a tincture of gold
flares in azure

and she has gone.
Dissolved
in distance.

Then. Now. Nothing.
Ecstasy of contemplation.
Meditation point, space

as full as an olive,
or the vase traversed
by heroes and heroines:

eternal frieze
upon the form
of emptiness.

3

Has all thought ceased?
It does seem the pale horizon
drains all feeling. What tune to play

to call her back, relocate?
How far in has she gone? Savanna,
that sad mix of she-oak and grasses,

yields to saltbush;
sandals slip, snap on gibber plains.
Nowhere to lie down. Wind pings.

Untouchable the spinifex,
and the hot sands,
in waves

as dunes run.
Arriving there, like some visitant,
her hair flows north-north-west

to south-east in undulating rills
already spreading herself
as I speak I know

she has gone beyond sand into rock country,
into violet shadows that cool fires

She has gone into
hard bright rainbow
silence of quartz country.

Loosened,
in silks of the unspoken,
she fans—

on valley slabs of altar stones
on blue and pink-veined tablets
on mountain shards of ocean bed, breast stroking . . .

4

Between the lion-coloured ranges—
No: camel-coloured (name what is here).
I say it for the place's sake,

though I'm not there, really
I am in her hair.
She is everywhere.

She has gone into the desert
that wilderness of sweets.
No one has walked there for ages.

A dreaming we make of it.
Honey-ant song rooted in porous
aridities. Hard won

the kiss that is prayer:
thus I project her
in my mind's eye

she eludes, I inscribe, in hopeful clarity.
Weather-vanes
are the shifting sands, sets of sets

And so I place her
ahead of the last vanishing
foot print, between

Sand and sky, rock and
sky, rock and sand:
Breathing her forward in star light.

5

Night. Us two apart now yet
happy wandering in self-recovery,
populating salt pans with memories:
                                You here:
your first child cries, newborn:
a cooing in tussocks, in moon-shadow,
suckling sounds in crevices, all paws;

The second born arriving in a rush,
the ground you are on a syllabic stretch
of time, the desert flooded

by the breaking of names, sounds cracked,
eggs turned out on rocks.
Sunshine yolks!

Procreational crust
in which ancestral syllables quiver, jet:
Submarine plains a lying down place of sound,

for underground travelling, genetic passage:
from one soak, its suction of time, to another,
from one increase place to another

swarm of stars, and the vomit
upward of spirit. Dizziness.
And then, slowly at dawn,

the passing of children's voices
with all of their beginnings,
(and yours too),

landing you alone
fecund among the grains
of the river's Milky Way.

6

       Me there:
an erection by stealth
of shadow, a growing
of my lotus for you.

A man lying along himself,
lizard to his thoughts,
morning pinks

the idea
of clear water and what it is not
flowing in him,

and perhaps her psalm,
though he cannot yet
presume unison.

As it is,
each day's furnace
incinerates despair.

Noon is
a cancellation of distance.
At dusk, smoke signals.

Song

So where did
your beloved go
lovely one?
Tell us which way
so we can find him

Part Three

Back

Returning inland
     seasons later
          a lizard waits for me.
Clatter in the kitchen.
     Length across the frying pan.
          I thought it's thump
and scuttle
     a bird on the roof
          it has striped rings
runs of sand down its tail.
          eyes like ants.

I tried to ignore it
     and it's off
          in timely spurts.
Wish I had
     suction pads
          tongue in groove
it tongues along the ceiling
     around the room
          and behind paintings
Black Cockatoo Dreaming
     and then under the big
          Ewaninga increase centre—
lizard with honey feet
     cheeky fat one
          plump as corkwood
and along the wire
     belly on the nail
          hanging the Men's Business
water hole
     until it's under the bark
          painting in the corner
where I am
     in the chair
          trying to doze.

Like water in water
        it flicks
                seconds away
from corner to corner
        ending up behind
                the dangling wok, head up,
cheeky as a dyybuk
        or hungry ghost
                trapped for good

Should I feed it
        almonds or watermelon
                Club chocolate or
that sliver of tomato?
        And how is it that
                once I'm back
in this room near the caravan
        I find myself
                putting memories
and fruit
        on the page
                slats and hopes
honey and rain—
        the pen driven
                like a dingo
the list swelling to a banquet
        kisses and raisins
                apricots, figs, tears,
all a lizard would not want . . .

these ideas
        scraps in the heat
                who knows, exactly,
what we need in captivity.
        there are quandongs
                galore outside
a lizard inside
        on a dry November day
                with a dimpled

breath in its throat.

Still as a promise
    I breathe
        glance away.
Gone.

Song

See—
beside a wall he stands
         shows himself
glancing through the lattice.

The bell bird relentlessly rouses her
The dark-chested one relentlessly rouses her

The bell bird fills her with madness,
The dark chested one fills her with madness . . .

Her desires she encloses with a fence,—
a thicket shuts her in like a fence.

Her desires are shut in by a fence,—
a thicket shuts her in like a fence

T. G. H. STREHLOW: *Song of the Kwalba Chief of Tera*

[52]

Found

Walk around the place
     naked in late sun.
          Fancy aloes and myrrh
under foot.
     This bush rose's
          mauve flower is a caress.

Someone (in love)
     planted those blazing
     marigolds by the basil,
beans among the corn.
     Plumped up, one day,
          those marrows will be.

All the wine of remembrance
     in my stroll
          wandering in the vineyard
of the old history,
     vegetative heat
          along my back
and buttocks:
     standing still
          in the heat build-up
a man might jerk off
     for the sun's sake,
          but close by
peering through the slats
     she holds him fixed:

His admiring his wife-to-be
     his new bride,
          his wife
his widow
     his wine press
          of past and prophecy

in memory psalm—
        in the moment he might have
                wasted himself
if seed can ever be
        wasted in a garden
                just at the thought
of his own disappearance
        he ripens
                senses her sight
and is picked
        all over again
                her sweat amongst leaves
thickens the throat
        like sandalwood,
                or eucalypt, yes
that young woman tree
        writhes as ever;
                his skin has nothing
on its white, her pallor
        that the sun spares,
                it just holds the light along one flank
winey sap in folds of the other
        and bellies out
                for him
in daylight and full
        shade, no worries:
                the mountain is in him.

I must have
        come back at
                the right time

Now will she tell
        from his voice
                his ideas, the scraps
of silence, or from
        his hold on her
                his listening
well?
        His plumb shadows

        sound her out
more calmly than
    hers down there
        somehow—

The test is if
    beyond this garden,
        they can
till the vineyards
    of this hard country
        breath
its double hum.

Song

Promise me
Daughters of Jerusalem,
swear by the gazelles
and roebucks of the wood
that you'll not rise up
or arouse love
until its time.

Sometimes, the Aranda word for red kangaroo can't be said.
Nor can the song be sung.
With its sacred word hidden in it.
The song that takes its name from that word.

So we speak, not of the original tongue itself, so much as of the
        kangaroo eating. *Ilkuma*, to eat.
He is on the luxuriant grass slope where he *ilkutjakalaka*, he
        descended eating.
Then he *ilkulb- ilkutjakalanadka*, descended slowly eating all the
        while.
Then he was down on the plain, where *Nala era ilkuetnalalbuka*,
He wandered on away from us eating on its way. Later, we might
        say, *Nala era ilkutjintjika*, here it browsed on the way up.

The modes of browsing. All in the word as active as the kangaroo
        eating.
We want a word for love in all its activities.

A word fat on its own music.

A term that has browsed all over.

Byron's Sky

What is happening
    in this time?
        I say to Thou,
Dear One
    (at risk of divine wrath)—
        OK, I say to rock
and to that passing cloud,
    to dust at my feet . . .

Like the pool at the bottom
    of the garden,
        let me sing
the way with Byron's
    Hebraic Melody
        its billowing chords,
and cupping of silence—
    As when you turn
        your eyes as doves
impatiently and
    interrupt me, again:
        for fear that I cast . . .

In turns we have stoned
    each other
        thrown over
calm in favour
    of lightning
        thunder
in our footsteps
    towards each other:
        Half bushed, storm happy.

Song

Look.
Who's this coming
out of the desert
like a pillar of smoke
with more incense, myrrh
frankincense than a merchant?

White Bird

A wide ground sheet,
a canopy of concepts
and still the poem won't

quite house the span
of dialogue, its reach
and raindrop promise.

Expectant, this season.
All humid mornings,
arid afternoons

dry as our tongues
after love making.
Whereas what I want

somehow,
are pomegranate stanzas,
apricot shadows

pressing through,
lines as strong as
the cedars of Lebanon;

a processional march
of pages that bridge
the first feasting

—genetic banquet—
with us in spirit here
like careless doves

without nests,
like poems in the air,
like this one

trying to soar
in peace above
its own space.

The white bird whirred and narrow tailed over me.
Arrowing the pale morning's crystal presence.

I looked up, I think, when it was overhead,
and saw its wings out there already gone.

A note—azure, with a flame in it—
pearled out beside the bird, mid-flight.

You could see the plump belly and throat,
and the note alongside body and tail shaft

as the two of them shot through the crystal
—the bird, the note, and the space between them

in unison as they travelled, until, at the right moment,
the note slipped free, leaving the space

that was ecstatically between it and the white bird
to fan open, and feather to ground like a poem.

3

Later, other birds arrived. Wagtail.
Currajong. And Warblers, one, two, three.

Ones I could name on the branch,
iron drum and barbecue hot plate.

Each flint eye on me, each beak pointedly
expectant, yes. For a moment there

I felt like St Frances, then I twigged:
I was sitting at Johnny Possum's providing place.

Finally they flew off, fed up with tea leaves.
'For by grace you are saved through faith.'

was not the text that pleased them,
anymore than it does me, when a note

goes its own way, and a feather comes down.
What more does a man need, when the space is right?

4

Walking back to the house, from Possum's caravan,
I paused at the young woman tree, admired a

gash, a ruby split in her back,
the juicy hardness of crimson welt and bejewelled

leakage that could have elevated that note,
among other things; I was under the high fork

where the fatty white creases run upward
to the sun, and downward in moonlight—

the crutch—I'll say that, this is physical,
it does not have to be poetry all of the time:

I stood under her and put my hand out
to the smooth lower parts, not patting

so much as resting my hand flat on flanks.
My palm came away snow white.

I wiped it to find my skin intact,
put the hand back on her and it was

all white again. Flour white, white wash
white; food and face cover white: she was a

natural invitation to body paint and mask.
Will I wear you as tree? Or can the tree

in me be you? Truth is, just then,
that time, I dusted my hands down

out of respect, thinking of the huge
space between me and a ghost,

even a holy one, a spirit as white, as
light as some trees and poems give off.

Song

At night in bed
        I reach for my love
seeking and not finding him
        saying to myself:
'I'll get up now
I'll go into the city,
roam streets and alleys
searching for the one I love'
        I looked
I searched for him
        I couldn't find him.
Patrolling
        the city the watchman
found me,
        and I said
'Have you seen
my beloved?'

Underground Rivers Running

If only you would speak to me
If only you would say something in this heat
If only you would pick up that stone and sing
                  pluck the bones out of your throat
                  hear my pauses between lines
If only you would laugh at the right time
                  digest my body well
                  go and stay with me always
If only you would leave me alone in you
If only you would see me for what I am by the river
                  hunt my gaze down each time
                  let my breath cool yours
                  your breath raise my body
If only the animals that pass between us spoke
If only the bird on my shoulder was uncaged
If only each of our words had the same root
If only our children would dance with each other
If only we had the same day to make the journey
If only you knew exactly what I knew
And what you know I believed absolutely, effortlessly

If only you could make my time flow only to music
If only every line of a poem could be danced
If only you had no greater need for sweetness than me
If only we could pass in and out of each other like water
If only all weather united us
                  and drought was a blessing to all
                  and my fire did not consume you or
                          yours me
If only your river filled my river with nectar
If only we could be the flood, and flood each other
If only there was no hope of drowning
If only underground rivers ran through us

Song

I'd taken my dress off:
how would I slip it back on?
My feet all washed,
—was I to soil them again?
Easing his hand
through the slats
my love made
all in me moan.
I rose to open
   to my love
and my hand dripped
   myrrh—
   my fingers wet with
   myrrh
on the handles of
   the lock
   the door
I turned with my own
   hands
and my love had
   gone.

In his wake my soul died.
I reached out and could not find him.
I called and he did not answer.

Upon the ground where I used to sit let me set my feet!
Upon my powdered soil let me set my feet!

With fire heated soil he covers himself
With a short stick he throws it over himself.

T. G. H. STREHLOW: *Kwalba Chief*

Corkwood psalms and sonnets

WOMAN

father, he said come to this garden singing
of honey, there are figs here that grow
out of rock, the white river bed flows with honey,
there is honeyflood time for all who dream,
and who respect their ancestors. This is what he said
before he dared to leave me alone here. Father
he has forsaken me, to me he said nothing, he sings
of nothing. I tremble like you, father, I also
shake as I speak about what has happened
to me, though he says nothing has happened, nothing.
At my feet there are melons as swollen as a nursing mother's
breasts. They are lemon-coloured. They have the pale,
soft skin that stretches his Achilles tendon but
I cannot eat them. They are bitter, they are food for horses.
father, the trees have died. I see black wood everywhere.
A fire has swept through this place, leaving no ash
but black wood. Father speak to me now, father help
me carry my grieving and deserving head indoors
where I might bathe myself at last,
and sleep my pride through this going
of my daughter, who hates him, the one
I had before him, before him.

> *Having gathered food let me give way to my passion !*
> *Let me, the maiden, give way to my passion!*

MAN

Love, you have located me up to a point
of nothing, except that emptiness is not nothing
it is all. The space in which we breathe is
the rose maze, even Sturt's Desert Rose. And
that heron, the last bird to scud on Yapalpa's pool,
came through her vast space by error
that was nothing, and yet everything.
From high up, she saw the iron roof

glinting, so she landed low-bellied
on the sheet of water that was metal.
Still, she has recovered, as we do, even after
metaphysical error. We do by pouring ourselves
forth again, and falling into such sharp
shaping of ourselves as this, navigationally.

WOMAN

Another day breaks and I am here on this rock, father.
The garden glowed a moment as I woke and now it burns.
I want to go indoors but I can't. I must wait.
When I manage to walk, lower down, the whirr
in the long grass is the snake turning on me.
I know this but do not see it. I see locusts, they whirr
also and the grass flicks with the dance of snakes.
father there is nothing to drink here. I am a broken cup.
Birds with ravishing necks do their flighty business
and flies, with their globular invincible eyes, pretend
to adore me. The ants that ascend my branch are in heaven,
damn them father. I would love the ghost gum if it would
hold me. There is another tree that I cannot name,
it is grotesque in its muscularity, it squats in the river bed
like seaweed seething in the wrong place, at the wrong time,
its base is as knotted as my stomach that I hold in,
father I am trying to be strong. The hot sun pinches
my nape. One cloud is floating towards me
from the east high up and white as hope.
but it's not her not my lost child.

      The crested rock pigeons
      Are coming near at hand.

MAN

Love, your father is there believe me
I am displaced but I am not him
I am rope to your miasma, your love call
to her is quicksand to me come
into my garden my love my wife
your kisses are sweeter than wine.
Your lamentations drive me to a fury of forms,
this vice of little song, whereas huge love endures fire

the desert is in your heart, the hidden spring
is in your mind not in his camps there are
no chimney stacks here, the ash is from grass fire
kind spinifex, your bloom is in quartz
here at Japalpa, where, even in rock, wound, bruise
and re-cognitions flower in the time Time has taken.

WOMAN

If the sap of black wood could give him milk
I would yield again, I would.
I would not hoard.
I'd be spices for him all over again. If he,
after laying me down between the strong posts of his bed,
could feed her the milk she won't let me give her,
—not now and maybe forever—
then I would bloom for him
from range to range in all seasons.
Father, when he stood before me this morning
I felt a chill. It was her, somewhere near.
A bird went tra tra la la la. Bellbird.
Kwepalepale, the others here call it in dance.
But my bellbird my first born my song is not here.
I remember her eyes. Their opals widen strata.
If I could sit here long enough, be bare in silence
long enough or have the strength to run
but where to? Sometimes I hear thunder in the hills.
I can stand up for that. But a roaring in me drags me down.
I can hear your voice, father, it's in the distance
as his is and whenever you spoke to me
about your life it was from a distance
that left you shaking before and after speech.
The same with me now. It does me
no good to speak and harm to be silent.
Does that mean we have light and
all that dark in common? Does each
word have to be crushed out of me?

The crested rock pigeons
are cooing plaintively

MAN

Leaning between the lines thus, peering through
the lattice of your hair, I'll love you in my poem.
Braid you by hand, write to you in candle light that burns
with the tightening of the throat and the silence
that assassins know, damn her damn you may God
save your father from his nightmares too:

The king comes and you rise
up to let him in, and from his height he lowers himself
to you again, on to your silken waters
where it matters that you have,
for a moment, opened in desperate
forgetfulness, and, as with a gorgeous summer melon,
I cut through to what I want,
to the food each watering place has.

WOMAN

He says I should try to turn the heat into a friend
of patience. He says that I should think in my heart of joining
it rather than keeping my ice in the shade. Melt, melt,
that is his message to me, father, as I am deeply inflamed.
If I lie myself down on this slab its hot plate is nothing
to my heart. I stroll barefoot on the baking riverbed,
scorching footprints behind me. Moving
between trees with my hair down,
grass fires start in my wake. And he,
he thinks me cold in myself as he walks beside me.
He is here everywhere, though he has abandoned me.
Father, I call you because my mother is dead.
Father, take care of them the one
I have and the one I have not.
May someone grant her a temple in her garden
where she can learn, as the rain falls on the pool,
the laws of sacrifice, if there are laws. And
teach her if you can from the cellar years
of your life still trembling in you,
teach her to forgive me. I gave her away
when I gave myself to him
I gave and I gave I am fat
I am a carcass father
I glisten with lice the crows love me
I call and I call all black beak.

Those sharp-crested pigeons
move about in every rocky height

MAN

Harp across my back, I can't play.
I can't save your music either
I'm on the other side of the river
with those parrots under the date palms,
I have crossed over to the feasting
and the fruit that sweetens.

My hope, my bright intention is that you
as you loosen for embarkation,
when you come to cross dead or alive
will find me there waiting, and cross-legged
finger painting the sand that you like
marking my words at the water hole
drawing a brooch for your hair
for the setting out, naked again, naked.

WOMAN

He presumes to know me
to pin me down in his poetry
to salt me down like some . . . hide!
as if my body shakes like yours
I have seen enough, he has said enough
sob until you're dead I can't
look at your photos once more
my camp is here father, in inland sea,
you must keep your trembling from me
I am a child here and he can't hear me either
sob until you're dead may you perish
in your own time father forgive me
this rock shelf I sit on is a shard
it is the split mountain's, a refugee
from burning forests ashened and
sunk, decomposed . . . deep as time can be.
Now on the surface, grains of sand
grate for water. The sky
above is a chasm for earth
earth is a cauldron for sky,
that's what this desert is it is
no garden when what has happened
has happened, you can't say or show any more
schisms, they fracture the face in a moment
passed already, already passed they are the most
worn statements of history we fall into and
and I am here without dance
my song splintered into solo ceremony.
Rocking with kindling, I thunder.
Cradling dawn embers I am lightning.
Cradling, I storm, father I storm
with him without him

Upon ground let me set my feet
Upon firm hard ground let me set my feet.

Having gathered food let me give way to my passion !
Let me, the maiden, give way to my passion!

The crested rock pigeons
Are coming near at hand.

The crested rock pigeons
are cooing plaintively

Those sharp-crested pigeons
move about in every rocky height

Upon ground let me set my feet
Upon firm hard ground let me set my feet.

T. G. H. STREHLOW: Kwalba

Part Four

Song

Love is as strong as death
> jealousy as cruel as the grave.
Its sparks flare
> in a fire eating country.

Late one night, as I was walking over the Todd river, where there are, these days, many deaths, I looked down from the bridge and saw something wonderful. They were a young couple, still unscarred by rough living.

In moonlight I saw them.
Two in the swag,
under the bridge.
His royal sleep.
Her hair flowing
over his happy arm.
A good cattle dog
guarding their marriage.

Much later, when I saw a cover illustration of the *Song of Songs* the connection was made. It showed a couple lying face to face, their eyes closed, their arms about each other. Naked from the waist up, and united below by bed clothes.

The original image was in alabaster, the lid of an Etruscan sarcophagus. In the lines of the carving you could see the *Song of Songs* flowing back to the death cults.

Stone

1

We come to the pool
To the lull of the gap
To the calm of deep water
And each floating seed

Of creation,
Where the stone we held
Is cast out there
Is sinking, is eddying down

To the seething mass,
Back to the ooze and the dark
At Yapalpa:
To the unborn, the uncreated

The still born, and the miscarriages
Of translation, to the dead
Breath and the birds
So far from the ocean.

2

The stone sinks and the sun
Lays violet along the range
The spinifex dies in rings
The heat subsides like bread

Yet still we are here
Quietly holding hands
As the stone goes down
And glinting in your hair

Is the evening star of the unborn.
It's bizarre: you are sobbing
And the pool is bloodied
But in my mind I am oddly full

—As if, in a spasm,
There is a brilliant whirr
Of dragon flies in the reeds
Of my heart. Once

Properly mated
Everything shimmers. See—
Phosphorescent union on water,
The shudder of falling.

3

We should have put it on our tongue.
We need to place it where it's
Warm and sweet in its own pool
Of savouring, gently sucked

At the pool's edge.
Listen. The frogs have started up
(hardly needs saying), invisibly
All eyes, wet as life itself

They are making one hell
Of a noise. Webbed feet. Bulbous
In the dark, vision forever
Looming for us, into us here

Waiting by the pool, at evening.
Stars are spawning. Love,
Look there, wonder there
Let things sink as they must.

4

It is not something in general,
It is this thing. The one star
The body of it gone
Light still on its way.

Is there a moon story
For such a pin-point of loss?
A dingo howls along the river.
Yelps from the litter rise

Into a stricken dome
Fall like droplets onto the pool.
Must be Pleiades Dreaming:
Daughters are crossing the sky.

Our constellation tilts.
Through the howling night
We sleep on grains of sand
In the pelt of time.

5

You feel we've lost a daughter
I'm not sure why but
My night is a lost son:
Neck cord, sinew of arm,

A strength behind and in me.
Weight of self—something
The body knows. The more
That is there, the more can

Fail, and disappear.
It is in me going down
This taut diminishment.
Plumb weighted, blue eyed.

Eagled in grip
Wings spread for hovering
And for gliding low
My crest swept upward

By the quick falling
My pride notwithstanding.
Some man in me swooning
And drowned.

6

All is quiet now.
The moon has set.
Frogs promiscuously still.
Frost on the ridge

Ice along your brow.
Mine feverish.
Is this it—
these polar extremes, after all?

I have iced up, you say.
In your sleep I lie awake
Trying to warm you up.
You have folded in while I

Have opened like a crimson
Desert flower.
Blood red, savagely
Celebratory in the face

Of your numb cold.
Sorry.
Oh the sorry business of your sleep.
'Boiling ice,' my pillow talk.

7

Love, should we go back
To the coast? Is the inland sea
Too far from home?

River trickles into sand.
Stepping stones scorch at noon.
The shade bakes. Strange dialectics.

Not so long back—the pool glowed.
We lost count of duck feathers.
Even the Bony Bream looked fat.

How is it you feel like
A grub, and I like a butterfly
When we made the same thing?

'Time running out'
Means one thing to you,
Another to me. Can we try

At least to imagine
The same stone? Again
There it goes

Flicked out across the water,
Heavily scudding once, twice
Then like a swollen petal

Subsiding, sinking out of sight
Gently going down
In that place

With everything unborn
Where the seething was,
En masse.

Song

I have come down
  into the nut garden
  among almonds
    fruits of the valley
    to see
    if the vine has flowered
    pomegranates budded

I am trembling
hardly knowing myself

The great sire, brandishing his short stick,
At his soft-soiled home scatters ash in all directions.

The Kwalba (chief) has wound his penis around himself, —
The great sire is tied up, his penis is tied up. . . .

. . . I am a married man, a truly married man
I am full of joy in my wife.

I am full of love for my wife;
I am a married man, a truly married man . . .

Threading the songs, trying to mend the broken songs, embracing the archaic language, only to kiss the bride through the veil, traducing,

Strehlow could in the end only make the best of loss after loss.

From Second Highest Dreaming Place in Town

The ground bursts with rock
       on each side of town
       but not along the river
              the sad river
From the hill
       I have the view
       of the caterpillar range
              and the Gap

Where the tjurunga were
       I can see down the road south
       straight as a telegraph pole
              or a good vow

Out West,
       the wedge of Mt Gillen
       and the resting place
              of the dingo pups

And beyond that
       the homely fact of Giles
       reading his Byron for breakfast
              and Strehlow

Born near his Range of Doom.
       As the eagle flies
       I can see some camps
              where Native Title People

Sleep. The quilt
       of yards and drains
       around them, the lanes
              where their kids play

Along the river
  the sad river.
  I knew a man, a kind American
    who was cursed:

He recorded from here
  bandages and snot, the bottles,
  he fancied he could hear
    the falling pitch

Of broken song.
  But that is the case
  some of the home truths
    along the sad river

Where the sand is as soft
  as it was for us
  at Love's Creek—
    even saying this much

Seeming to score
  voyeuristic
  or retrospective points
    makes me a mongrel

At the Dingo Cafe
  puts me out of bounds
  in another way
    sad right along

This river song.
  And after it—
  what?

Throat

To have warm wide breasts
    like that woman
        crossing the highway:
letting the young men go ahead
    gangly with fire wood
        knowing as they do
exactly how many breaths
        of daylight are left
in this glorious, glowing
    suspense of things
        before night—
the way the country
    used to tell you
        everything
if you waited right:

she steps out
    arms akimbo,
        four dingo pups in a row
jostled along at her bosom,
    the fold of each
        flapping ear
dusty fur at her throat
    perambulating
        all scent and muzzle
    and there being no
        spirit there
    to call out, to warn her
        of the giant snarl of
          Roaring Road Train.

Stills

*

Babel Bore is
Where the camels were.
That the sound,
Seed syllables make
Breaking up?

*

In the beginning
Was the deed. We fall
In the face of it. All
Sugared up

*

The song
The song goes down
In flames. Words
Consumed in the desert

*

Back into Egypt
the dogs howl.
Red fish, heart
of the song,
leapt into Israel

*

A tune
a note from
these river people
and we'd have the old
melody of honey

*

Only the black
knitted woollen hat
Port Lincoln Parrot colours
keeps you warm in this easterly

*

Canticles are lice
I lay me down by the river
Pray a man won't
flagon me to death

*

That ink or blood
on the tail of his shirt?
The young fellah in front
is drunker. Splattered one
the good shepherd

The Same Air

In the darkened room, the round
of them, the single file, the hands—
I dreamed of a meditation hall
where a sea once was
a centre for the circle of clasps
the hands placed—so—
not on the belly but fattening calm
on the diaphragm, and then

then you see them come
you see them go in the round
of the single file, a man, a woman
another man with his tread
his unique measure at the wheel
in meditation and the morning
in hope of their clearing

A bell rang. Who is it for?
The door to the zendo is open
it's the desert of the soul in there
that's what it's for, it's there for the round
of people in the darkened air
the single file in the air of their time.

We're all in here, there, and everywhere
preparing for death if we're not dead
visiting the dead who are here now
and carting the stones of the dead
from the thickened air of the shower room.
Remember? I Remember. We went there.

We stood in the round of the barrelled room,
far from here with one cold hand
pressing it on the concrete wall
sweating and seeking not to fall
unclasped and clasping
the memory of those single files . . .

The bell rings. Back in the dream,
in coming towards the round of them
a line of figures in the Australian dawn
I approach a hall that is more than a hall
a movement of the morning light
a fading flame as the day comes
with the breath that snuffs the candle
the last bell is as thin as a rib.

It is for the sitting, that bell.
Sesshin. They will go down.
Will ease themselves onto the floor
arranging their legs—touch, perhaps, their hair
breathing again to ready for death
they will be as one in a tomb
living each breath for the day again
in single file, in the air of their time

The life of the mind, and in Poland
in castings of thought, in normality
in retreats that become an inland sea
in bouts of sitting that blur
in the scheme of things that transcend
in the emptiness of hope, as in love
in the figure and in the shadow
on the wheel, here and there.

Single Notes

1. Quandongs, quartz, desire.

2. A late new moon, the oldest river's oldest song.

3. Harp and didge. My hand and your breath.

4. So much distance they whirly whirly together.

5. Cicatrices deeper than culture.

6. Feasting is spawning, wasp in the beef wood coconut husk.

7. Have you eaten? The world tastes of nuts.

8. The dust storm's marital row with rust.

9. Left my body Outback. Struck it rich.

10. Salt, your hair, wine of clear water. I dissolve here.

11. Country swarms with thought until you reach the cave.

12. What must the dove celebrate? Ask the snake.

13. No escaping the blade of concepts. I just can't draw it out.

14. Wire rattles the chook house. As good a song as any.

15. Even the lice-ridden crow knows how to shake things off.

16. Say it to each morning breeze: marriage is sitting together.

17. Flint in my palm. Blood ceremony.

18. Listen for you, hear myself, try to return to sleep.

19. Poem of feast and celebration, sucked at the bone table.

20. Country of bleached remains, stories buried in sand.

21. Each note rising succeeds the other. Green the tail of its mate.

22. Water drops and the light swelling melody.

23. One wave's scoop leaps to the crest of the other. Rock music.

24. Lock me up for holding to this: rock is the same as water.

25. Free me to say nothing when underground travelling.

26. Paddy melons and partitas. Figs and fugues.

27. Try to end the poem. Make rain.

Song

I am trembling
hardly knowing myself